Music for the Millennium: The Eighties

A Woman In Love 22
Against All Odds (Take A Look At Me Now) 43
Always On My Mind 26
Endless Love 34
Every Breath You Take 29
I Think We're Alone Now 51
(Just Like) Starting Over 16
Money For Nothing 54

On My Own 46
One Moment In Time 64
Private Dancer 38
The Lady In Red 58
The Wind Beneath My Wings 68
The Winner Takes It All 13

Music compiled by Peter Evans and Peter Lavender
Song background notes by Michael Kennedy

All text photographs courtesy of
Rex Features International

Cover photograph of Madonna
from Katz Pictures

Edited by Pearce Marchbank

Text researched and compiled by Heather Page
Book design by Pearce Marchbank and Ben May
Picture research by Nicki Russell

Printed in the United Kingdom by
Page Bros Ltd, Norwich, Norfolk

Exclusive Distributors:
Music Sales Limited
8-9 Frith Street,
London W1V 5TZ, England.
Music Sales Pty Limited
120 Rothschild Avenue,
Rosebery, NSW 2018,
Australia.

Order No. AM92361
ISBN 0-7119-4437-7
This book © Copyright 1997
by Wise Publications

Unauthorised reproduction of any part of
this publication by any means including
photocopying is an infringement of copyright.

This publication is not authorised for sale in
the United States of America and/or Canada

Your Guarantee of Quality
As publishers, we strive to produce every book
to the highest commercial standards.
This book has been carefully designed to minimise
awkward page turns and to make playing from
it a real pleasure.
Particular care has been given to specifying acid-free,
neutral-sized paper made from pulps which have not
been elemental chlorine bleached. This pulp is from
farmed sustainable forests and was produced with
special regard for the environment.
Throughout, the printing and binding have been
planned to ensure a sturdy, attractive publication
which should give years of enjoyment.
If your copy fails to meet our high standards,
please inform us and we will gladly replace it.

Music Sales' complete catalogue describes thousands
of titles and is available in full colour sections by
subject, direct from Music Sales Limited.
Please state your areas of interest and send a
cheque/postal order for £1.50 for postage to:
Music Sales Limited, Newmarket Road, Bury St.
Edmunds, Suffolk IP33 3YB.

Visit the Internet Music Shop at
http://www.musicsales.co.uk

Wise Publications
London/New York/Paris/Sydney/Copenhagen/Madrid

We met in a ploughed field.
DIANA SPENCER ON MEETING
PRINCE CHARLES

Great fun, bouncy and full of life…
I'm amazed that she's been brave
enough to take me on.
PRINCE CHARLES ON HIS ENGAGEMENT
TO DIANA SPENCER

I asked Sarah some weeks ago and
Sarah actually said 'Yes', which
surprised me. She did say also…
'If you wake up tomorrow morning
you can tell me it was all a huge joke'.
PRINCE ANDREW ON HIS ENGAGEMENT
TO SARAH FERGUSON

'ET Phone Home'
CATCH-LINE FROM
STEVEN SPIELBERG'S
SMASH HIT OF 1981

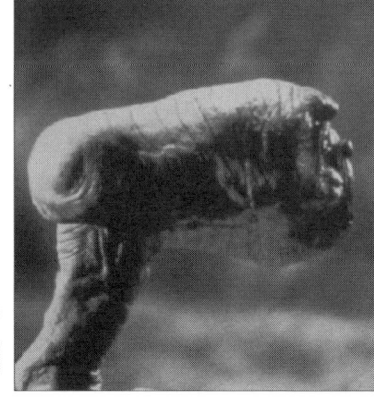

For the first time in history,
a Bishop of Rome sets foot
on English soil.
THE POPE ON HIS VISIT
TO BRITAIN, 1982

Should we ask the Falklanders how they feel about a war?
FOREIGN SECRETARY FRANCIS PYM TO MARGARET THATCHER, 1982

QUEEN ELIZABETH 2
SOUTHAMPTON
WEDNESDAY 12TH MAY 1982
SHIP SAILS AT
FOR
FALKLAND ISLANDS
ALL CREW SHORE LEAVE EXPIRES 1200
ALL PASSENGERS TO BE ABOARD AT
ALL IDENTITY CARDS TO BE SHOWN 1200
DONT CRY FOR ME ARGENTINA

If anybody has a go back home about the quality of youth in our country, they ought to have seen these guys. They were absolutely tremendous.
JEREMY MOORE, ENGLISH COMMANDER, ON THE TROOPS CAPTURING PORT STANLEY, ENDING THE WAR IN THE FALKLANDS

The next anniversary one would hope would be that of ten years as Prime Minister.
MARGARET THATCHER ON TEN YEARS AS LEADER OF THE TORIES, 1985

I'm not frightened...
I don't believe the American people
are frightened by what lies ahead.
Together we're going to do what
has to be done. We're going to
put America back to work again...
RONALD REAGAN'S ACCEPTANCE SPEECH
AFTER DEFEATING JIMMY CARTER, 1980

All attempts to destroy democracy by terrorism will fail.
MARGARET THATCHER AT THE TORY PARTY CONFERENCE JUST AFTER THE IRA BOMB AT THE GRAND HOTEL, BRIGHTON, 1984

She showed extraordinarily few outward signs of shock, and still fewer of fear...it was as if such terrible deeds were only to be expected from her wicked enemies, and they must not be seen, by even so much as the flicker of an eyebrow, to have touched her.
HUGO YOUNG IN 'ONE OF US' ON MRS THATCHER THE DAY AFTER THE BRIGHTON BOMBING

Today marks a visit that is perhaps more momentous than any which have preceded it, because it represents a coming together not of allies but of adversaries.
PRESIDENT REAGAN ON GORBACHEV'S VISIT TO WASHINGTON TO SIGN THE TREATY TO REDUCE THEIR NUCLEAR ARSENALS, 1987

I have recovered. I feel fine.
If I'm a medical miracle,
then I'm a happy one.
70-YEAR-OLD PRESIDENT REAGAN
AFTER THE ASSASSINATION ATTEMPT
BY JOHN HINCKLEY

You ain't seen nothing yet.
PRESIDENT REAGAN ON HIS
RE-ELECTION IN 1984

I find he's not only a barbarian,
but he's flaky.
PRESIDENT REAGAN ON
COLONEL GADDAFI OF LIBYA

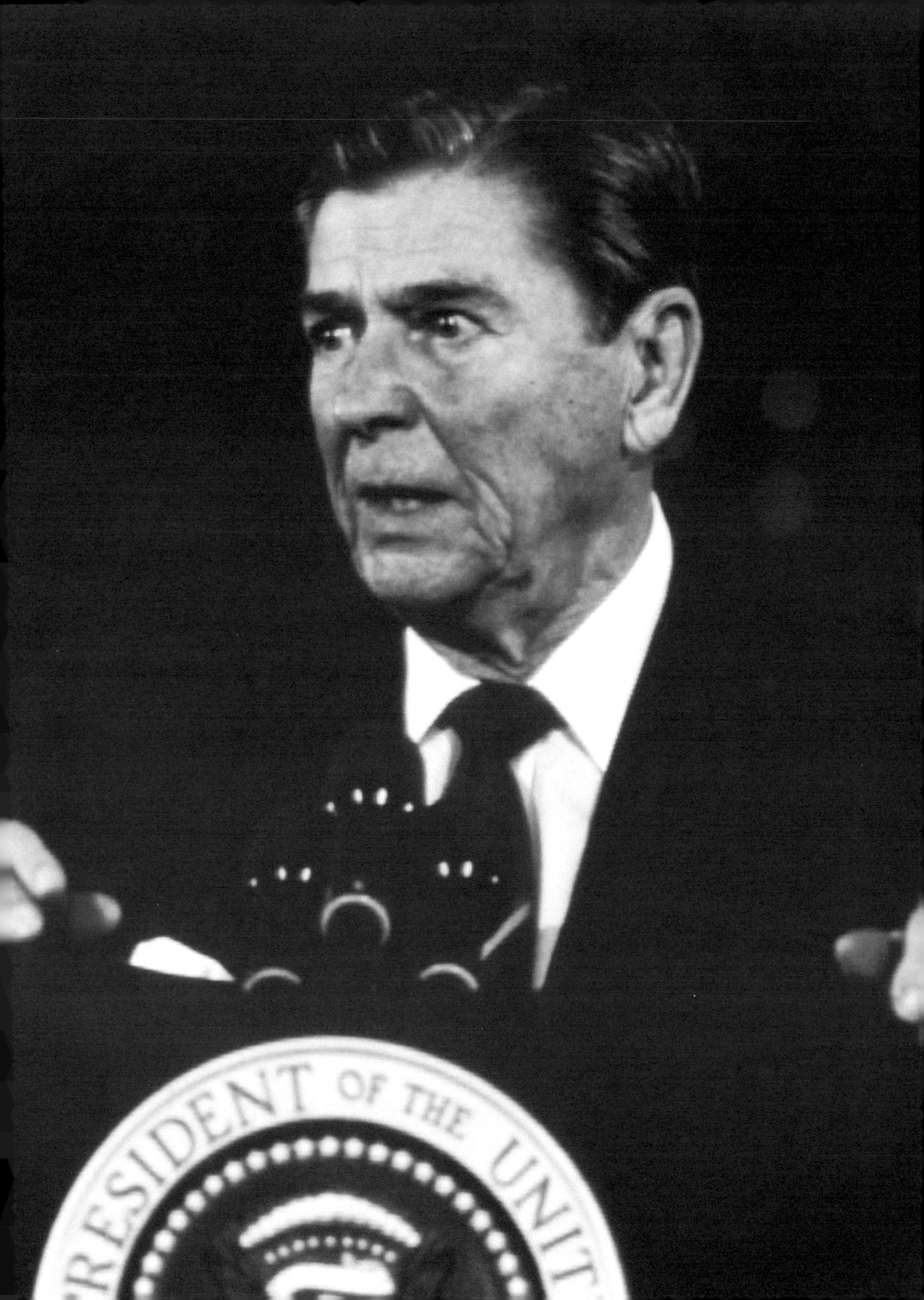
PRESIDENT OF THE UNIT

Just give us the fucking money.
BOB GELDOF, LIVE AID, 1985

She said it was a small token for what you've done, it must have been very hard work. I said, 'Not as hard as getting into this thing'.
BOB GELDOF ON HIS SUIT AFTER BEING KNIGHTED BY THE QUEEN

It's the largest outpouring of love and affection that this city's ever seen.
MAYOR KOCH OF NEW YORK ON THE RETURN OF THE AMERICAN HOSTAGES FROM IRAN

This man did one thing that we really appreciated as we sat on the floor in our underwear on the day of Christmas Eve. He gave us hope.
AMERICAN HOSTAGE DAVID JACOBSEN, FREED IN BEIRUT AFTER TERRY WAITE'S INTERVENTION, 1986

I'm still here, of course, because I believe that I have definitely got a job to do. I'm receiving local protection, although I realise that there is no protection that can be 100% secure.
TERRY WAITE BEFORE DISAPPEARING AND BEING TAKEN HOSTAGE IN BEIRUT, 1987

I must tell you that what we've got is an attempt to substitute the rule of the mob for the rule of law.
MARGARET THATCHER DURING THE MINERS' STRIKE, 1984

The trade union movement of Britain has left this union isolated.
ARTHUR SCARGILL, 1985

These are the last days of Thatcherism.
LABOUR LEADER NEIL KINNOCK ON THE EVE OF THE 1987 ELECTION WHICH THE TORIES WON

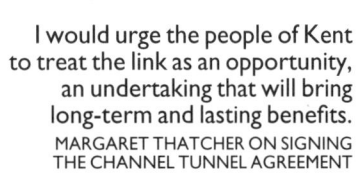

I would urge the people of Kent to treat the link as an opportunity, an undertaking that will bring long-term and lasting benefits.
MARGARET THATCHER ON SIGNING THE CHANNEL TUNNEL AGREEMENT

I would like to make it clear that England is committed to Europe, to the Common Market idea.
MARGARET THATCHER, 1980

Most of all, people should go and hear something about Gandhi. He really was the most remarkable little fella.
RICHARD ATTENBOROUGH AFTER HIS FILM 'GANDHI' HAD WON EIGHT OSCARS, 1983

It's going to be different because it's going to try to cater for some viewers in ways that they're not catered for at the moment. I'm thinking particularly of young people for whom we are going to do a lot... we're going to do some programmes that will drive mums and dads out of the room.
JEREMY ISAACS OF THE NEW CHANNEL 4, 1982

All five of us will be co-hosting *Good Morning Britain* during the coming year... a programme we hope will be full of surprises for you, and sometimes, no doubt, for us too.
ANNA FORD ON THE LAUNCH SHOW OF THE ILL-FATED TV-AM

I feel elated! Two and a half hours... it's gone quickly and... I enjoyed it!
SELINA SCOTT OF BBC TV'S 'BREAKFAST TIME' AFTER THE FIRST BROADCAST

We've had a call from a lady worried about a hurricane tonight. Don't worry, there isn't going to be one!
BBC WEATHERMAN PRIOR TO THE WORST HURRICANE IN BRITAIN FOR 200 YEARS, 15 OCTOBER 1987 (SEE OVERLEAF)

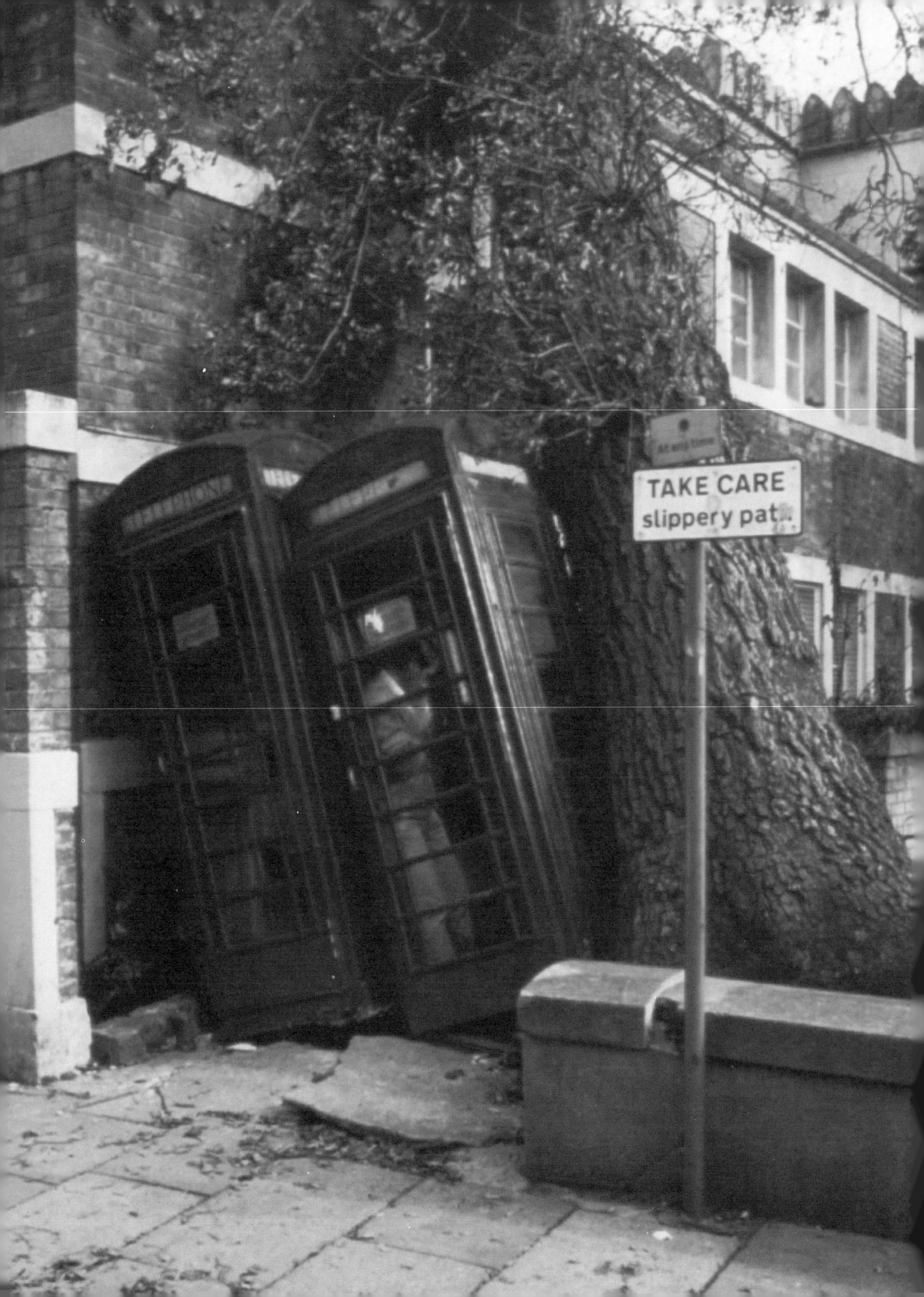
TAKE CARE
slippery pat...

The Winner Takes It All

Words & Music by Benny Andersson & Bjorn Ulvaeus.

© Copyright 1980 Union Songs AB, Stockholm, Sweden for the World.
Bocu Music Limited, 1 Wyndham Yard, Wyndham Place, London W1 for Great Britain & Eire.
All Rights Reserved. International Copyright Secured.

The most successful Scandinavian pop group of all time, ABBA sprang to international fame in 1974 when they won the Eurovision Song Contest. A stream of hits continued. In Autumn 1980 came the eighth of nine No.1s in Britain, 'The Winner Takes It All'. The song proved to be the group's fourth and last American hit, reaching eighth place.

I don't wan-na talk a-bout things we've gone through, though it's hurt-ing me, now it's his-to-ry. I've played all my
arms think-ing I be-longed there, I fig-ured it made sense, build-ing me a fence, build-ing me a
kiss like I used to kiss you, does it feel the same when she calls your name. Some-where deep in-
talk if it makes you feel sad, and I un-der-stand you've come to shake my hand. I a-po-lo-

cards   and that's what you've done too,   nothing more to say,
home,   thinking I'd be strong there,   but I was a fool,
side   you must know I miss you,   but what can I say,
gize   if it makes you feel bad   seeing me so tense,

no more ace to play.   The winner takes it all,   the loser standing
playing by the rules.   The gods may throw a dice,   their minds as cold as
rules must be obeyed.   The judges will decide   the likes of me a-
no self confidence.   The winner takes it

small   beside the victory,   that's her destiny.
ice,   and someone way down here   loses someone dear.
bide,   spectators of the show   always staying low.

[1] I was in your   [2-3] The winner takes it all,   the loser has to fall,
                                   The game is on again,   a lover or a friend,

Eb7/G
Abm
Db
1
it's sim - ple and it's plain, why should I com - plain. But tell me, does she
a big thing or a small, the win - ner takes it all.
2
D.%. al Coda
I don't wan-na
CODA
Gb
Bb7/D
Ebm
all.
Eb7/G
Abm
Db
The win - ner takes it all.
Gb
Bb7/D
Ebm
Eb7/G
Abm
Db
Repeat and fade

(Just Like) Starting Over

Words & Music by John Lennon.

© Copyright 1980 Lenono Music.
Administered by BMG Music Publishing Limited, Bedford House, 69-79 Fulham High Street, London SW6 3JW.
This arrangement © Copyright 1995 BMG Music Publishing Limited.
All Rights Reserved. International Copyright Secured.

When The Beatles disbanded, John Lennon's spiritual and personal partnership with Yoko Ono ushered in a new phase of his creative talent. Tragically, on 8th December 1990, John was killed outside the Dakota Building in New York. '(Just Like) Starting Over' had just been released. It proved to be the first posthumous number one hit for its composer.

Lyrics:
Our life together is so precious together. We have grown. We have grown. Although our love is still special, let's take a chance and fly away somewhere alone. It's

Moderately, with a strong beat

[A] been too long since we took the time. No one's to blame. I know time flies so
day we used to make it, love. Why can't we be mak-in' love nice and

[Bm] quick - ly!
eas - y?

But when I see you, dar - lin',
It's time to spread our wings and

it's like we both are fall - ing in
fly. Don't let an - oth - er day go

Bm
E
love ___ a - gain. It - 'll be just like start - ing
by, ___ my love. It - 'll be just like start - ing
A
A+
o - ver, start - ing
o - ver, start - ing
A
To Coda
1.
A+
o - ver. ___ Ev - 'ry
o - ver. ___
2.
G
Tacet
Why don't we take off a -

Am
D7
lone, take a trip some-where far,
G
Em
far a-way. We'll be to-geth-er all a-
Am
D7
lone a-gain, like we used to in the
D. S. 𝄋 (lyric 1) al Coda 𝄌
G
E
D/F♯
E/G♯
ear-ly days. Well, well, dar-lin'. It's

Our life together is so precious together. We have grown. We have grown.

A
A+
Al - though our love is still spe-cial,
F♯m/A
A7
let's take_ a
D
Dm
chance and_ fly a - way___ some - where.____
Repeat (vocal ad lib) and fade
A
A+

A Woman In Love

Words & Music by Barry Gibb & Robin Gibb.

© Copyright 1980 Gibb Brothers Music.
All Rights Reserved. International Copyright Secured.

The Bee Gees aren't just a talented group of singers who write their own music. They write hit songs for others as well. On 4th October 1980 Barbra Streisand entered the hit parade with 'A Woman In Love', written by Barry and Robin Gibb. The song reached No.1, and remained there for three weeks.

Moderately Slow

1. Life is a mo-ment in space,—
   when the dream is gone—— it's a lone-li-er place.——
   I kiss the morn-ing good-bye,—— but down in-side——

2. With you e-ter-nal-ly mine,——
   in love there is—— no meas-ure of time.——
   We planned it all at the start,—— that you and I——

B7 Em Am
you know we nev-er know why. The road is nar-row and long
live in each oth-er's heart. We may be o-ceans a-way
Em Am Cmaj7 D7 G
when eyes meet eyes and the feel-ing is strong.
you feel my love I hear what you say.
Dm G C G C
I turn a-way from the wall. I stum-ble and fall, but I give you it all.
The truth is ev-er a lie. I stum-ble and fall, but I give you it all.
B7 Em B Em B
I am a wom-an in love and I'd do an-y-thing
Em B Em B Em
to get you in-to my world, and hold you with-in. It's a

right — I de-fend o-ver and o-ver a-gain. What do I do?

D.S. al CODA

CODA — What do I do?

I am a wom-an in love — and I'm talk-in' to you. — I know how you feel, —

what a wom-an can do. It's a right I de-fend o-ver and o-ver a-gain.

I am a wom-an in love, and I'd do an-y-thing to get you in-to my world, and hold you with-in. It's a right I de-fend o-ver and o-ver a-gain.

Always On My Mind

Words & Music by Wayne Thompson, Mark James & Johnny Christopher.

© Copyright 1971, 1979 Screen Gems-EMI Music Incorporated & Rose Bridge Music Incorporated, USA.
Screen Gems-EMI Music Limited, 127 Charing Cross Road, London WC2.
All Rights Reserved. International Copyright Secured.

It's a good start for any song when Elvis Presley records it. 'Always On My Mind' was the fourth Presley hit of 1972. Ten years later, Country and Western great Willie Nelson took the song back into the Top 40. More recently it has attracted the attention of The Pet Shop Boys. You can't keep a good song down.

Slow and steady

1. May-be I did-n't treat you quite as good as I should have, May-be I did-n't love you quite as of-ten as I should have;
2. May-be I did-n't hold you all those lone-ly, lone-ly times, and I guess I nev-er told you I'm so hap-py that you're mine;

Lit-tle things I should have
If I made you feel

26

said___ and done, I just nev-er took the time.___
sec-ond best, girl, I'm so sor-ry I was blind.___

You were al-ways on my mind; (You were al-ways on my mind.) you were al-ways on my___ mind.   mind.

Lead:

Tell_____ me, tell me that your sweet love___ has-n't

died. _____ Give _____ me, give me one more chance to keep you sat-is-fied, _____ sat-is-fied.

mind;

you were al-ways on my mind.

Every Breath You Take

Words & Music by Sting.

© Copyright 1983 G.M.Sumner. Magnetic Publishing Limited, London W1.
All Rights Reserved. International Copyright Secured.

Former Newcastle teacher Gordon Sumner found fame and fortune as a musician, singer and songwriter under the name Sting with his group Police. He wrote the song 'Every Breath You Take', which topped the British charts for four weeks, and the American charts for eight, in 1983.

Ev-'ry breath you take, ev-'ry move you make, ev-'ry bond you break, ev-'ry step you take,

Dsus
Em
D7sus
G
I'll be watch-ing you.
Ev - 'ry sin - gle day
Em
ev - 'ry word you say,
ev - 'ry game you play
C
D
Dsus
G
ev - 'ry night you stay,
I'll be watch-ing you.
C
C/B♭
Am7
G
Oh, can't you see
you be - long to me.

How my poor heart aches with ev-'ry step you take. Ev-'ry move you make Ev-'ry vow you break, ev-'ry smile you fake ev-'ry claim you stake, I'll be watch-ing you.

Since you've gone I been lost without a trace, I dream at night I can only see your face. I look around but it's you I can't replace, I feel so cold and I long for your embrace. I keep crying baby baby please.

C
D
Em
G
D.S. al Coda
CODA
Em
C
Oh can't you
Ev - 'ry move you make Ev - 'ry step you take,
D
Dsus
Em
I'll be watch - ing you.
D7sus
G
I'll be watch - ing you.

Endless Love

Words & Music by Lionel Richie.

© Copyright 1981 PGP Music & Brockman Music, USA.
Warner Chappell Music Limited, 129 Park Street, London W1.
All Rights Reserved. International Copyright Secured.

The 1981 film success Endless Love, a steamy and ultimately tragic story of teenage love, featured an attractive, impassioned title song composed by Lionel Richie, who sang it with Diana Ross. Their recording of 'Endless Love' stayed nine weeks at the top in America. It reached seventh position here in Britain.

Moderately Slow

1. My love— There's on-ly you in my life—
2. Two hearts— Two hearts that beat as one—

The on-ly thing that's right— For-
Our lives have just be-gun—

My first love— You're ev-'ry breath— that I take—
ev - er— I hold you close— in my arms

Eb/F F F/Bb Bb F/A
You're ev - 'ry step I make And
I can't re - sist your charms And
Ebmaj7 Eb/F F Bb F/A Gm Dm/F
I I want to share all my love
love I'd be a fool for you I'm
mf
Ebmaj7 Eb/F F Bb Ab6/Bb Abmaj7/Bb Ab/Bb
To Coda
with you no one else will do And your eyes
sure you know I don't mind 'Cause
Eb Eb/F F 1 Bbmaj7 F/A Gm Dm7/F
they tell me how much you care Oh
you you mean the
Ebmaj7 Dm7 Cm7 Eb/F
yes you will al - ways be My End - less

Bb
Love
2
Bbmaj7
F/A
Gm
Gm/F
Ebmaj7
Dm7
world to me Oh I know I found in
Cm7
Eb/F
Bb
you My End - less Love
3
Eb
Eb/F
F
F/Bb
Bb
Eb
Eb/F
F

F/Bb
Bb
D.S. al Coda
Oh And
CODA
Ab6/Bb
Ebmaj7
And yes
Eb/F
F
Bb
F/A
Gm
Gm/F
Ebmaj7
You'll be the on - ly one
Oh no I can't de-ny
f
ff
Dm7
Ebmaj7
Dm7
Ebmaj7
this love I have in-side
And I'll give it all to
Dm7
Cm7
Cm7/F
Bb
you my love
My End-less Love
mf
Eb
Eb/F
F
F/Bb Bb
p

As well as turning out a stream of hits for his own supergroup Dire Straits, guitarist/composer Mark Knopfler found time to write the title track of Tina Turner's best selling album 'Private Dancer', whose world-wide sales exceed 15 million. Tina started life as Annie Mae Bullock - the name change certainly did her no harm.

Private Dancer

Words & Music by Mark Knopfler.

© Copyright 1984 Straitjacket Songs Limited.
Rights administered for the world by Rondor Music (London) Limited, Rondor House,
10a Parsons Green, London SW6 4TW.
All Rights Reserved. International Copyright Secured.

1.4. Well, the men come in these plac- es,
2.3. *(See additional lyrics)*

and the men are all the same. You don't look at their

fac- es, and you don't ask their name.

on the wall. } I'm your pri- vate danc- er, a danc- er for mon- ey; I'll
ask their name.

F♯m7
Esus
E
do what you want me to do. I'm your pri - vate danc - er, a
Gmaj7
1
G♯m7♭5
D♯°
D7
danc - er for mon - ey, and an - y old mu - sic will do.
D.S.
2.4.5.6.7 etc.
1st time D.S.S. 2nd time repeat & fade
F♯m7
G♯m7♭5
C♯7♭9
F♯m7
Bm7/E
an - y old mu - sic will do; I'm your
3
G♯m7♭5
D♯°
D7
F♯m7
an - y old mu - sic will do.

Deutsche marks or dollars; A-merican Express will do nicely, thank you. Let me loosen up your collar. Tell me, you want to see me do the shimmy again?

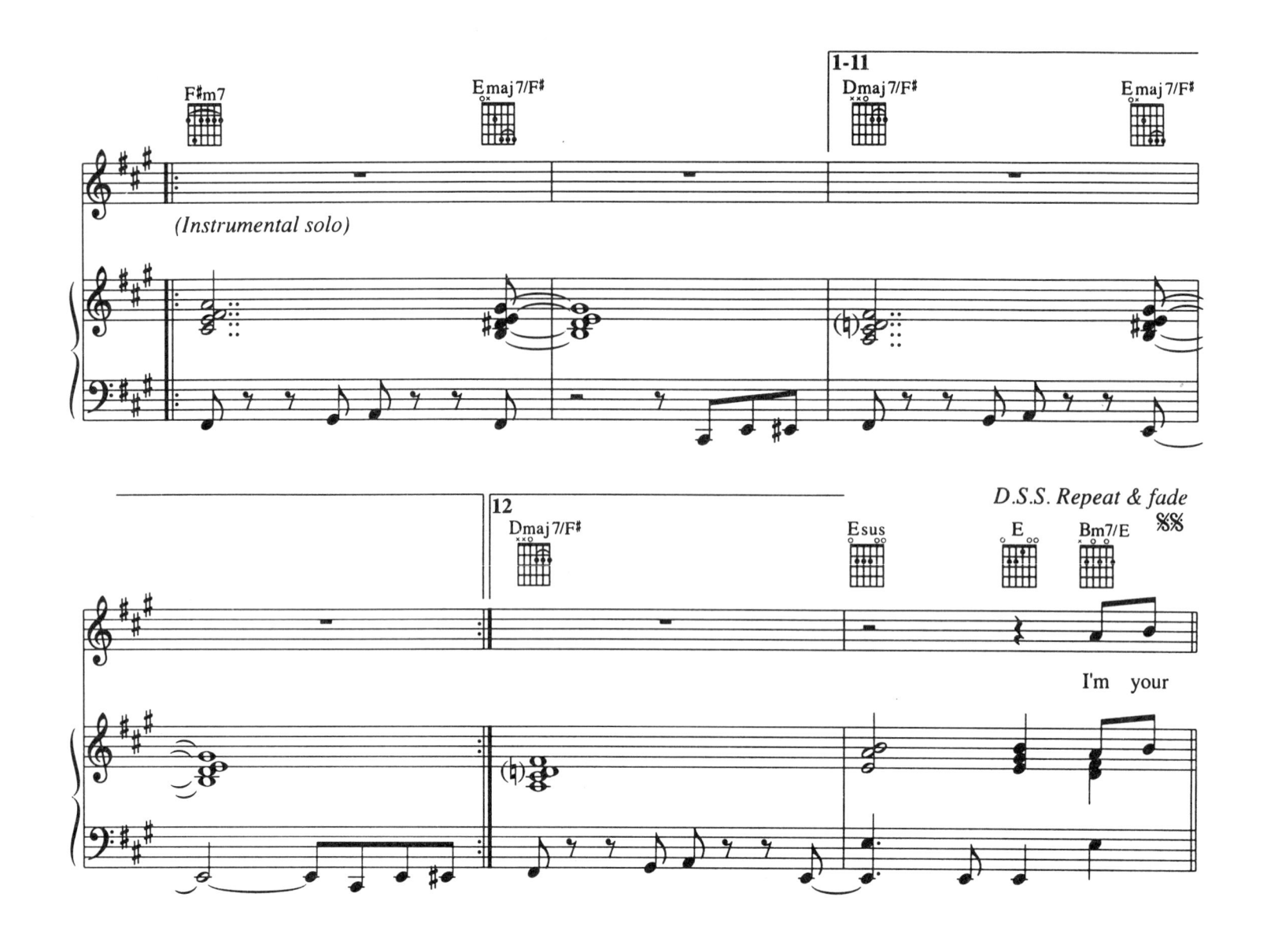

Verse 2:
You don't think of them as human.
You don't think of them at all.
You keep your mind on the money,
Keeping your eyes on the wall.

(To Chorus:)

Verse 3:
I want to make a million dollars.
I want to live out by the sea.
Have a husband and some children;
Yeah, I guess I want a family.

Against All Odds
(Take A Look At Me Now)
Words & Music by Phil Collins.

© Copyright 1984 Effectsound Limited/Golden Torch Music Corporation/Hit & Run Music (Publishing) Limited,
25 Ives Street, London SW3 (75%)/EMI Music Publishing Limited, 127 Charing Cross Road, London WC2 (25%).
All Rights Reserved. International Copyright Secured.

The 1984 film Against All Odds featured a title song, nominated for an Academy Award (and recipient of an Ivor Novello award), written by Phil Collins, lead singer and drummer with Genesis, and a megastar in his own right. The song entered the British charts in April 1984 and reached second position.

1. How can I just let you walk away, just let you leave without a trace? When I (2, 3. see additional lyrics) stand here taking ev'ry breath with you; Ooh, You're the only one who really knew me at all. So take a look at me now,

Well there's just an empty space, ⎯ And there's nothing left here to remind me, just the mem-'ry of your face, ⎯ Well take a look at me now. ⎯

Well there's just an empty space, ⎯ And you comin' back to me is against the odds, ⎯ and that's what I've got to face. ⎯

2. How can you just walk away from me
   When all I can do is watch you leave?
   'Cause we shared the laughter and the pain,
   And even shared the tears.
   You're the only one who really knew me at all.

3. I wish I could just make you turn around,
   Turn around and see me cry.
   There's so much I need to say to you,
   So many reasons why.
   You're the only one who really knew me at all.

On My Own

Words & Music by Carole Bayer Sager & Burt Bacharach.

© Copyright 1985, 1986 New Hidden Valley Music & Carole Bayer Sager Music. Rights for New Hidden Valley Music administered by MCA Music Limited (25%)/Rights for Carole Bayer Sager Music administered by Warner Chappell Music Limited (50%)/Windswept Pacific Music Limited (25%).
All Rights Reserved. International Copyright Secured.

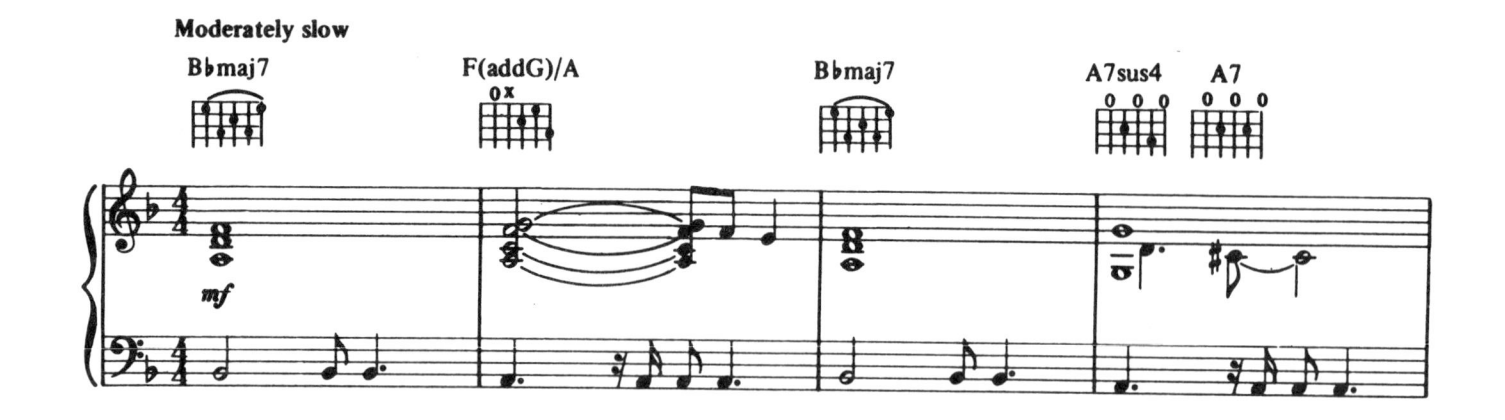

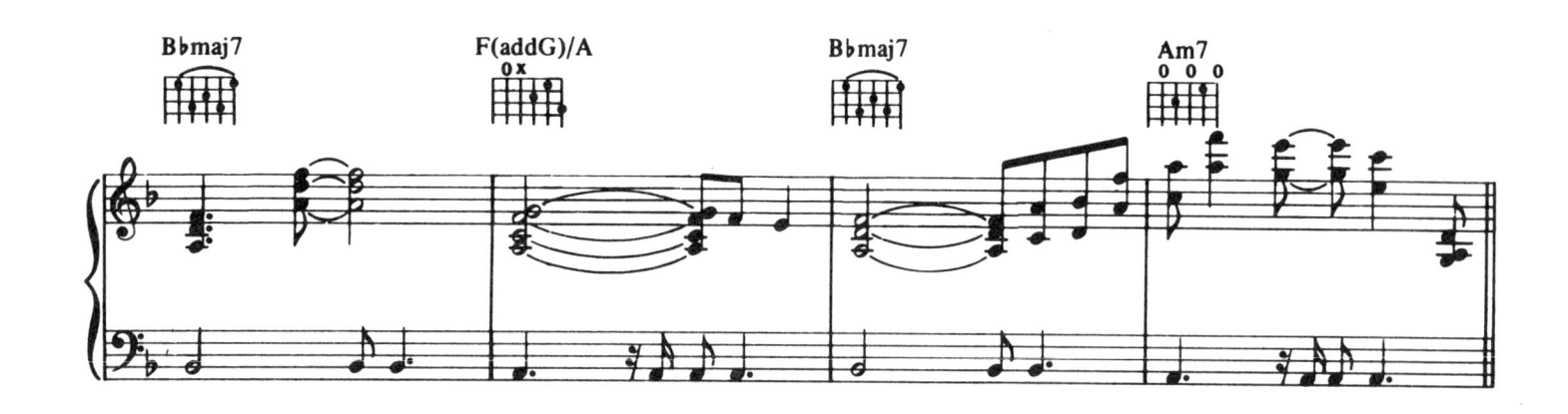

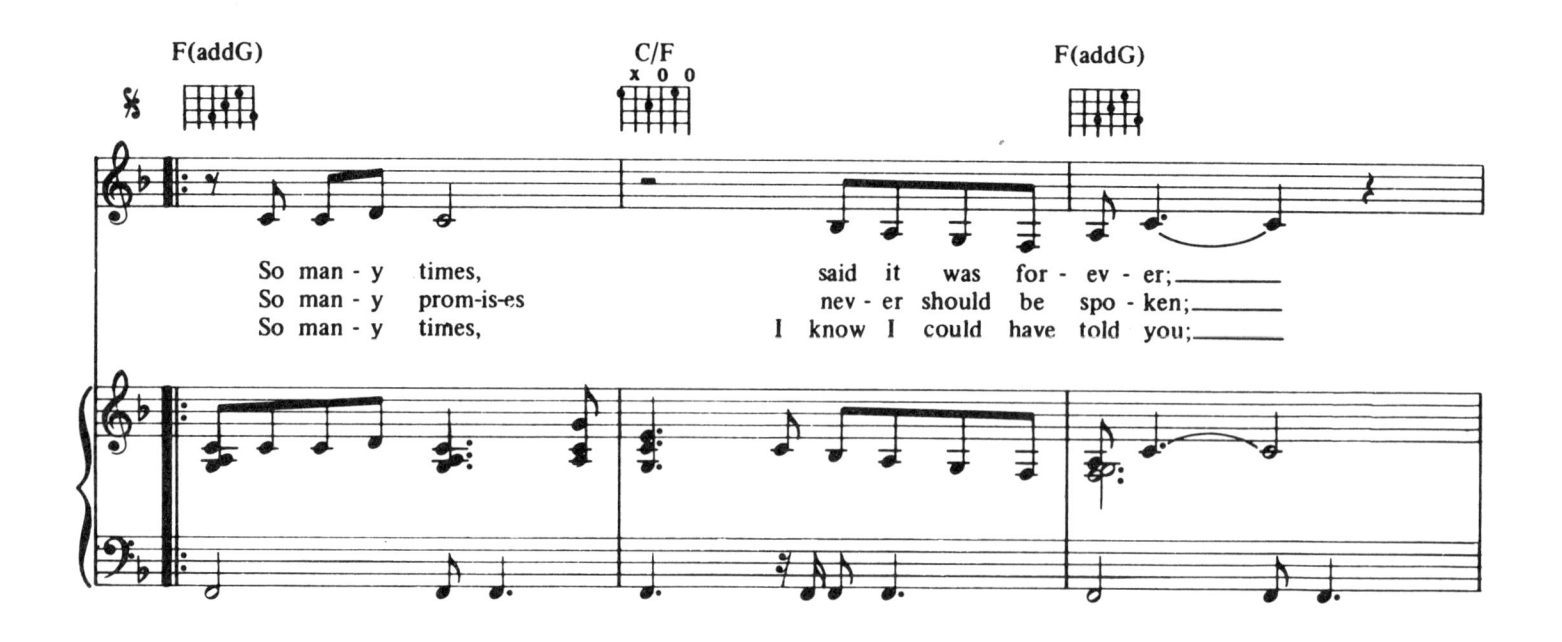

Burt Bacharach, one of the most widely admired of all popular songwriters, teamed up with the impressive and versatile lyricist Carole Bayer Sager in 1986 to write 'On My Own' which became a powerful hit recording on both sides of the Atlantic for the duo of Patti LaBelle (real name Patricia Holt) and Michael McDonald, reaching second place in the British charts.

So many times, said it was for-ev-er;
So many promises nev-er should be spo-ken;
So many times, I know I could have told you;

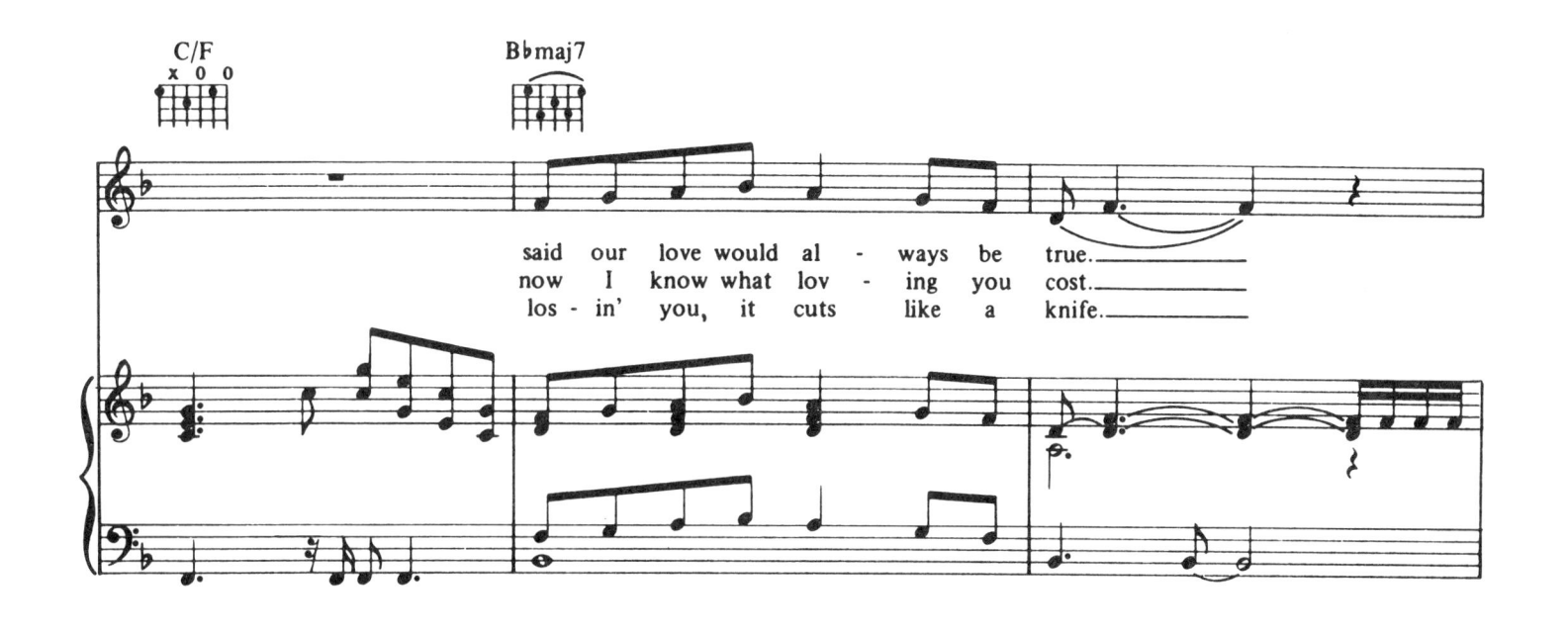

C/F   **B♭maj7**

said our love would al - ways be true.
now I know what lov - ing you cost.
los - in' you, it cuts like a knife.

B♭6(no 5th)   **B♭maj7**   **B♭6(no 5th)**   **B♭**

Some - thing in my heart al - ways knew I'd be
Now we're up to talk - in' di - vorce and we
You walked out and there went my life; I don't

F(addG)/C   *To Coda* ⊕

ly - ing here be - side you.   On my
were - n't e - ven mar - ried.   On my
want to live with - out you.   On my

Gm7/C ... F(addG)/C

own, _____ on my own,
own, _____ once a- gain,
own, _____ on my own,

1. Gm7/C

____ on my own.
____ one more
____ on my

2. Gm7/C ... **F**

time. _____ By my- self;

F(no 3rd)
Bbmaj7
C/Bb
C
no one said it was eas - y,
F
F(no 3rd)
Bbmaj7
but it once was so eas - y.
Gm7
3fr.
Well, I be-lieved in love, now here
Am7
Dm7
I stand; I won-der why

I'm on my own. (Group) On my own, on my own.

Repeat and fade (vocal ad lib on repeats)

Coda: own, on my own, on my

own, by my-self. (Group) On my

I Think We're Alone Now

Words & Music by Ritchie Cordell.

© Copyright 1967, 1987 Longitude Music Company, USA.
Windswept Pacific Music Limited for the UK & Eire.
All Rights Reserved. International Copyright Secured.

California's Tiffany (Darwish) made a name for herself singing in America's shopping malls. She scored a No. 1 hit on both sides of the Atlantic at the age of 16 with her version of the Ritchie Cordell classic 'I Think We're Alone Now' in 1987/88. She enjoyed two weeks at the top in America and three in Britain.

Brightly

1. Child-ren be-have, that's what they say when we're to-geth-er. And watch how you play. They don't un-der-stand and so we're run-ning just as fast as we can,

2. Look at the way we got to hide what they're do-ing. 'Cause what would they say, if they ev-er knew and so we're

holding on to one another's hand, trying to get away into the night, and then you put your arms around me as we tumble to the ground and then you say, I think we're alone now, there doesn't seem to be anyone around I think we're alone

— now, the beat-ing of our hearts is the on-ly sound.

I think we're a-lone now, there doesn't seem to be an-y-one a-round. I think we're a-lone — now, the beat-ing of our hearts is the on-ly sound.

Repeat to fade

Money For Nothing

Words & Music by Mark Knopfler & Sting.

© Copyright 1985 Chariscourt Limited/
Rondor Music (London) Limited/Magnetic Publishing Limited, London.
All Rights Reserved. International Copyright Secured.

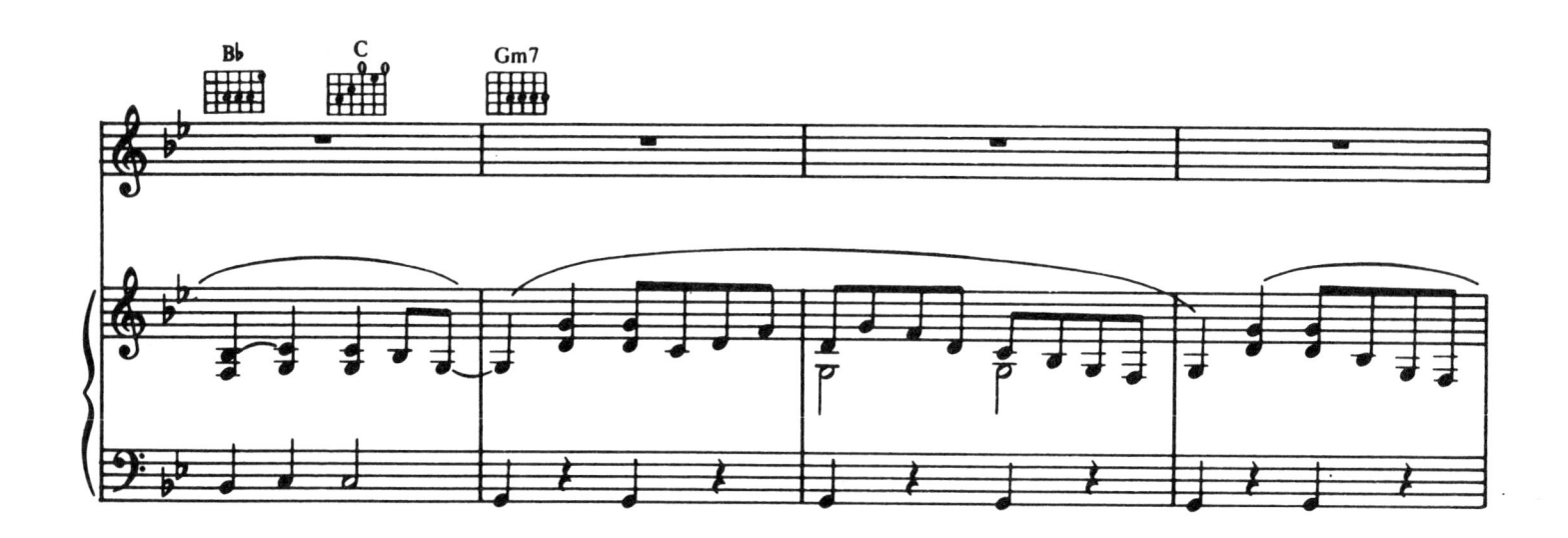

'Money For Nothing' achieved fourth place in the pop charts during 1985. It had the singular distinction of being written by the leaders of two of the most successful groups of the time - Mark Knopfler of Dire Straits (who had the hit) and Sting (Gordon Sumner) whose band, The Police, was to break up in the same year.

Medium rock ♩ = 138

1. Look at them yo-yo's that's the way to do it
5. (𝄋) I shoulda learned to play the gui-tar
7. (𝄌) Look at them yo-yo's that's the way to do it

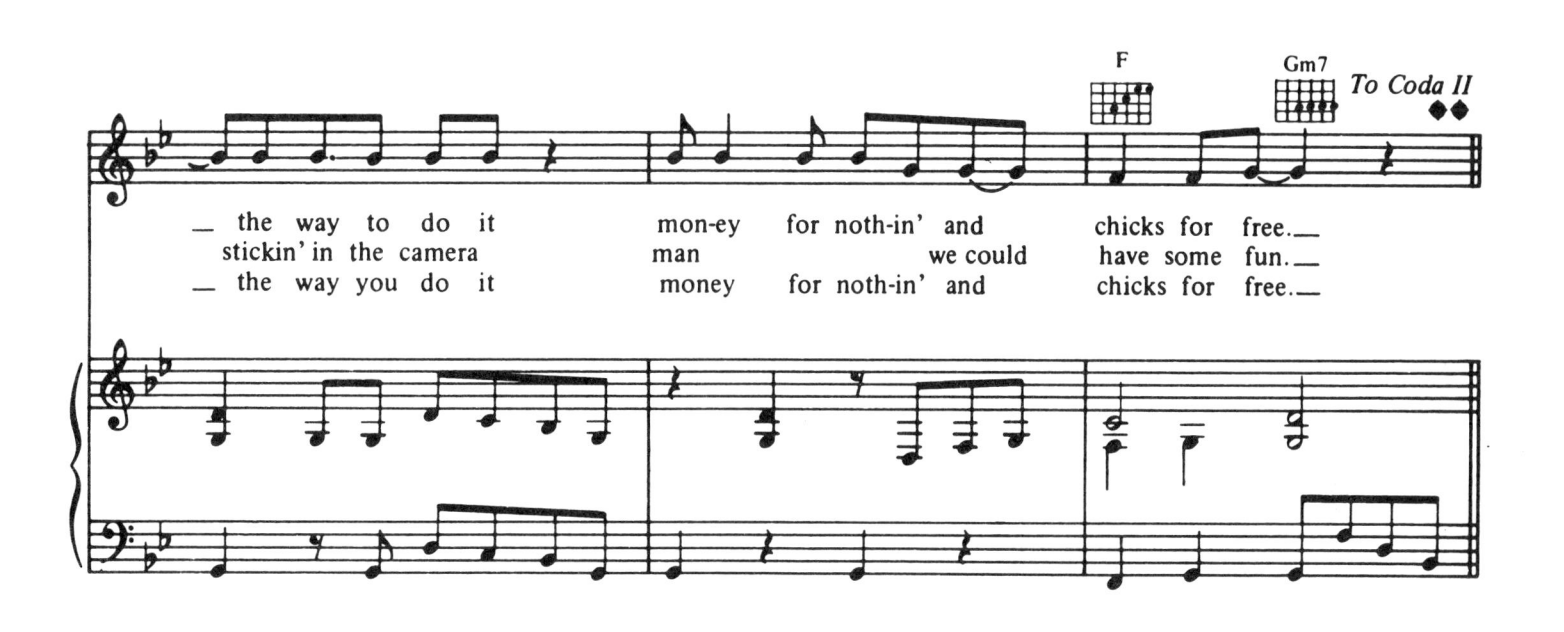

| | Gm7 | | Bb | C | Gm7 | |

play the gui-tar on the M. T. V. that ain't workin' that's
I shoulda learned to play them drums look at that she got it
play the gui-tar on the M.. T. V. that ain't workin' that's

| | | F | Gm7 *To Coda II* |

— the way to do it mon-ey for noth-in' and chicks for free.
stickin' in the camera man we could have some fun.
— the way you do it money for noth-in' and chicks for free.

| Gm7 | | C | Gm7 |

2. That ain't workin' that's — the way you do it lem-me tell ya them
3. See that little faggot with the ear-ring and the make up yeah buddy that's
4. INSTR. to Chorus
6.(%) And he's up there he's making Hawaiian noises bangin' on the bongos like a

guys ain't dumb___ may-be get a blis-ter on your lit-tle fin-ger
his own hair that lit-tle fag-got got his own jet air plane
chimpanzee that ain't workin' that's the way you do it

may-be get a blis-ter on your___ thumb.___
that little faggot he's a millionaire.
money for nothin' and chicks for free.

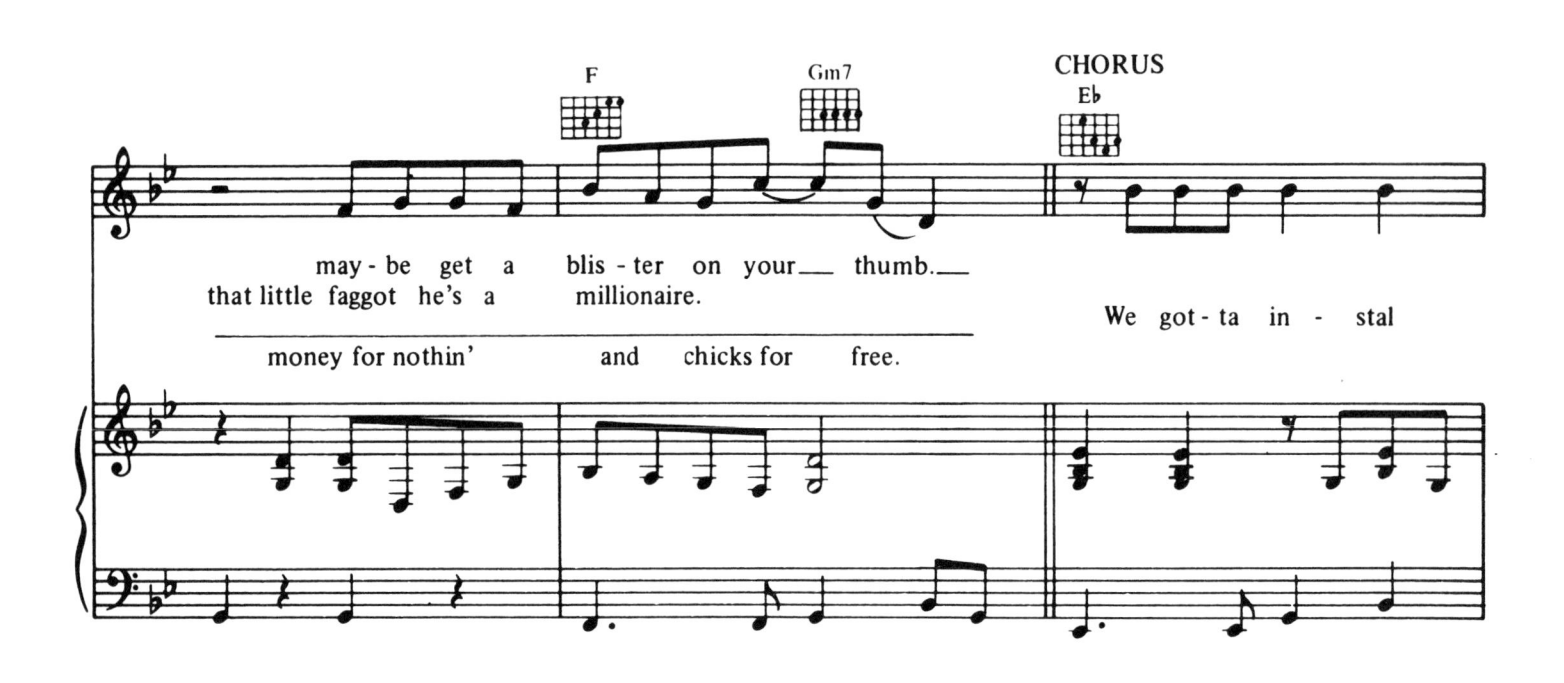

We got-ta in-stal mi-cro-wave ov-ens cust-om kit-chen de-liv-er-ies___ we got-ta move these

C
D
E
To Coda I
re-friger-a-tors we got-ta move these co-lour T.-V's.
CODA I
E
D.S. al Coda I
D.S. al Coda II
CODA II
Gm7
mo-ney for noth-in'
C
Gm7
Bb
C
Gm7
chicks for free
mo-ney for noth-in'
F
Gm7
Ad lib to FADE.
and chicks for free.

The Lady In Red

Words & Music by Chris de Burgh.

© Copyright 1986 Rondor Music (London) Limited, 10a Parsons Green, London SW6.
All Rights Reserved. International Copyright Secured.

The Irish singer and songwriter, Argentine-born Chris de Burgh (real name Christopher Davidson) had had hits before but his self-penned 'The Lady In Red', inspired by his wife, proved to be his major success, reaching top position in the charts in 1986, and remaining a pop classic ever since.

1. I've never seen you looking so lovely as you did to-night,
   never seen you looking so gorgeous as you did to-night,
   I've never seen you shine so bright,
   I've never seen you shine so bright,
   mm mm mm mm.
   you were amazing.
   I've
   I've

never seen so many men ask you if you wanted to dance,
never seen so many people want to be there by your side,

they're looking for a little romance, given half a chance,
and when you turned to me and smiled, it took my breath away,

and I have never seen that dress you're wearing, or the
and I have never had such a feeling, such a

highlights in your hair that catch your eyes,
feel-ing of com-plete and ut-ter love,

I have been blind.
as I do to-night. The

lady in red

is danc-ing with me, cheek to cheek,

there's no-bo-dy here, it's just you and me, it's where I wan-na be, but I hard-ly know this beau-ty by my side,

I'll ne-ver for-get the way you look to-night.

2. I've way you look to-night,

Gm/F
Gm/E
Cm7
I never will for-get
F7
Bb
the way you look to-night.
Bb/D
Ebmaj7
F
x3
Bb
The la-dy in red,
x3
Bb/D
Ebmaj7
F
Bb
my la-dy in red.

After a successful career in Britain, the London singer/songwriter Albert Hammond moved to America. He continues to write hits for stars of the calibre of Tina Turner and Whitney Houston, whose version of 'One Moment In Time', written with John Bettis, became the US Olympics theme. It topped the British charts in Autumn 1988 for two weeks.

One Moment In Time

Words & Music by Albert Hammond & John Bettis.

© Copyright 1988 Albert Hammond Incorporated, USA.
Empire Music Limited, 27 Queensdale Place, London W11 (50%)/
Warner Chappell Music Limited, 129 Park Street, London W1 (50%).
All Rights Reserved. International Copyright Secured.

Moderately slow

(1.) Each day I live I want to be a day to give the best of me. I'm only one but not a - lone, my fin - est day is yet un - known.

heart for ev'- ry gain, to taste the sweet I faced the pain. I rise and fall yet through it all this much re - mains.

be the ve - ry best, I want it all, no time for less. I've laid the plans, now lay the chance here in my hands.

(2.) I broke my { I want } one mo - ment in

Give me

time when I'm more than I thought I could be. When all of my dreams are a heart-beat a-way and the ans-wers are all up to me. Give me one mo-ment in time, when I'm rac-ing with des-ti-ny, then in that one mo-ment in time, I will feel, I will feel e-ter-ni-ty.

3º Segue

* 3° continue
Am
Fmaj7/G
Gsus4
G
(3.) I've lived to feel e - ter - ni -
C
Ab
C
ty. You're a win - ner for a life - time,
Ab
G
if you seize that one mo - ment in time, make it
Ab
rall.
a tempo
Db
Bbm
shine. Give me one mo - ment in time when I'm
Ebm
Ab/C
Gb
Ab
more than I thought I could be. When all of my dreams are a

heart-beat a-way and the ans-wers are all up to me. Give me

one mo-ment in time when I'm rac-ing with des-ti-

ny. Then in that one mo-ment in time, I will

be, I will be, I will be free.

I will be, I will be free.

The Wind Beneath My Wings

Words & Music by Jeff Silbar & Larry Henley.

Larry Henley of The Newbeats wrote (with Jeff Silbar) 'The Wind Beneath My Wings' and the song was twice a hit: first in 1983 as a Grammy winning country hit for Gary Morris, and six years later as Bette Midler's sole British hit when it reached fifth position, while making it to No.1 in the States.

© Copyright House Of Gold Music Incorporated & Bobby Goldsboro Music Incorporated, USA.
Warner Chappell Music Limited, 129 Park Street, London W1.
All Rights Reserved. International Copyright Secured.

Slowly flowing, in 2

It must have been cold there in my shad-ow,

to nev-er have sun-light on your face.

You've been con-tent to let me shine,

[Am(add B)] you al-ways walked the step be-hind. [D7sus4] [D7]

[G(add A)] I was the one with all the glo-ry, [C] [D/C]

[G(add A)] while you were the one with all the strength, [D/C] [C]

[Am(add B)] on-ly a face with-out a name, [D7sus4] [D7]

I never once heard you complain.

Did you ever know that you're my hero,

and ev-'ry-thing I'd like to be?

I can fly high-er than an ea-gle,

'cause you are the wind beneath my wings.

It might have appeared to go unnoticed that I've got it all here in my heart. I want you to know I know the

D7sus4
D7
Am(add B)
truth:
I would be noth -
D. S. al Coda
D
B/D♯
in' with - out you.
Coda
Gmaj9
C
D/C
wings.
You are the wind
Am7/D
D7
G(add A)
C
D/C
be - neath my wings.
mp
p